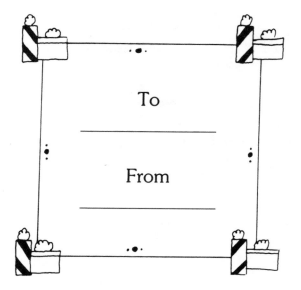

To

_____

From

_____

My Mother
Is the Best Gift
I Ever Got

My Mother
Is the Best Gift
I Ever Got

Children on Mothers

David Heller

Villard Books　New York 1993

Villard Books is a registered trademark of Random House, Inc.

Library of Congress Cataloging-in-Publication Data
Heller, David.
My mother is the best gift I ever got : children on mothers /
David Heller.
p. cm.
ISBN 0-679-41757-5
1. Motherhood. 2. Mother and child. I. Title.
HQ759.H457 1993
306.874'3—dc20   92-27271

Manufactured in the United States of America

3 5 7 9 8 6 4 2

First Edition

Introduction

If you want to find out how important and influential mothers are, just ask their children. Or even better, just listen to their children. Youngsters talk about their mothers all the time, and they frequently do so in a spirit of praise and adoration. Of course, sometimes youngsters will offer a gentle critique of their mothers and other moms too. Because four- to ten-year-olds spend so much time with their mothers, they have a special perspective on motherhood and on how children really see their mothers.

In this collection of wisdom and humor about motherhood, children reflect on the place of their mothers in their lives and in the world as a whole. They begin with what being a mother is like, and they share their observations on how mothers typically talk and behave. The children describe their own mothers, and their love for Mom comes through loud and clear. The children have some fun with mothers too, as they share original Mother's Day cards, depict Mom's housekeeping and culinary habits, discuss what the tabloids might have to say about Mom, and offer much, much more.

Through all the amusing quips and comments, this collection is a salute to mothers and to their great contributions to the life of any child. The children help us to remember that while a mother performs all kinds of roles in and out of the family, nobody else could possibly fill her role. A mother is a very special person indeed.

—DAVID HELLER, PH.D.

My Mother
Is the Best Gift
I Ever Got

Reflections on Motherhood

"Motherhood is fun if you have the time and
the children for it."
Bradley, age 10

"Mothers are like the Beatles because they got long
hair and they are pretty old."
Nathan, age 10

"Motherhood ain't for me. . . . I'll probably
be a father."
Dick, age 7

"The best thing about motherhood is nobody ever
makes you quit. You can do it as long as you want."
Jenny, age 8

"Motherhood is fattening, but I would still
recommend it."
Marie, age 9

"Mothers used to be little girls but then they got grown-up all of a sudden."

Roberta, age 8

What Are Mothers For?

"They give you your allowance and then
borrow it back when they run out of
money at the market."
Arnold, age 10

"Mothers are there in case nobody else
will marry you."
Jay, age 5

"Mothers keep the love and the chocolate chip
cookies coming."
Vern, age 7

"Mothers are the ones that bring you into the world,
but that only happens after God has put
the finishing touches on you."

Julio, age 9

Concerning What the World's First Mother Was Like as a Mom

"She would hire a dinosaur for the day and use it to sweep up the cave."

Dick, age 7

"The first mother was probably a lot like the mothers that you get now, except I don't think they had hairdressers in those days."

Gary, age 9

"I think her name was Mary and she was the type of mother who didn't get in the way of her son if he wanted to perform miracles or something like that."

Karen, age 8

"I bet she made her kids clean their room, and that's why we have to do it to this day."

Sam, age 8

"The mother gets the thermometer out, and if you pass the test, you get a free vacation day from school."

Sam, age 8

What Do All Mothers Have in Common?

"All mothers shop till they drop."
Tamara, age 8

"Quite a few mothers have big feet, but I'm not going to name any in particular."
Josh, age 8

"Many mothers are too overprotective. Like my mother won't let me go to Texas and ride a bronco in the rodeo because she thinks I might get hurt. Can you believe that?"

Tom, age 10

"Mothers listen pretty good, but fathers will talk your ear off."

Sharon, age 9

"Many mothers take too long to shower, and a kid has to wait forever."

Ryan, age 7

"They are all full of love and their children have red faces because of it."

Janet, age 10

"Mothers always kiss you when you come home from school.
Even if your friends are right there."
Sam, age 8

How Does a Mother Learn How to Be a Mother?

"Mothers learn by mistakes. . . . So I would say they get to learn quite a bit."
Shari, age 9

"Having a baby is a big education by itself."
Karen, age 8

"Learning mother things kind of runs in the family."
Alison, age 8

"Maybe they read the book: *How to Be
a Cool Mother.*"
Wayne, age 9

"Their children teach them everything, but some of
those mothers are slow learners."
Brian, age 7

Essential Qualities of All Good Mothers

"You have to be smart. . . . Because you never know, you might have to figure out whether your little tyke is tellin' the truth or fibbin'."
Cheryl Ann, age 9

"Good mothers tell the best jokes about animals."
Daniel, age 7

"A good mother knows what the answers are to your homework, but she gives you the chance to find them out first."

Jenny, age 8

"A good mother is somebody who doesn't yell at you for getting a bad grade. She understands, because maybe she got a bad one sometime too."
Roberta, age 8

"Good mothers make homemade orange juice—
not the easy kind."
Maura, age 9

"They let you stay home sick from school—
with no questions asked."
John, age 10

"Good mothers have smiley children."

Ronnie, age 6

"Mothers are always trying to find out how you are feeling.
They care about inside stuff like that."
Cheryl Ann, age 9

Mothers and Fathers: How Are They Different?

"*He* doesn't usually wear high heels."
Billie, age 6

"My mother doesn't snore much."
Kimberly, age 7

"Mothers try to make your life softer; fathers try to make you tougher. But fathers are big phonies. My father is just a big couch potato."

Mitchell, age 8

"Mothers are at home more, and that's good. My mother spells better than my father, and it makes my life a lot easier."

Kevin, age 8

"Mothers teach you your manners. Fathers don't know about that."

Bryant, age 5

"Mothers and fathers are different in every way . . . except for how much they love you."

Carey, age 7

Typical Motherisms
(Maternal Sayings)

" 'Don't get into arguments with other children. You
don't see your father and me arg—uh . . . uh . . .
Well, a child your age shouldn't be
arguing, anyway.' "
Arnold, age 10

" 'Stop playing with that Super Mario guy.' "
Ryan, age 7

" 'Eat all your vegetables. Even the ones that taste like wax.
They're good for you.' "
Jim, age 8

" 'I'll never fit into that size again.' "
Janet, age 10

" 'I know I shouldn't have this superrich milkshake,
but hand it right over to me.' "
Clark, age 9

" 'Clean your room. You have a half an hour. Hurry
up. The clock is running.' "
Gretchen, age 6

What Mom Was Like Before She Was a Wife and Mother

"She shaved her legs more often."
Kimmie, age 10

"She spent most of her time in the woods looking for animals."
Sam, age 8

"I heard she was real whiny when she was a baby."
Dick, age 7

"Right before she was a mother, she and my dad were planning my mean and stupid older brother."
Garo, age 6

"She fought a lot with her brother and sisters and that's how she got to be an expert about families."
Roberta, age 8

Mom's Greatest Personal Strength

"I count on my mother for love, and she never
lets me down."
Debra, age 9

"The thing that I'm amazed at is that she always
knows the answers on *Jeopardy*."
Alison, age 8

"She can mash garbage with her bare hands."
Jim, age 8

"She can keep loving and kissing all day long. Even if it's after nine o'clock."

Theresa, age 6

"Her greatest thing is roast beef and potatoes. Um, um, good."

Hal, age 7

"She has a good personality. That's why I picked her."

Del, age 6

Mom's Biggest Weakness

"She can't play basketball. She should learn. That way, I could practice my jump shot against her."
Robbie, age 8

"I never once saw her beat up any bullies."
Julio, age 9

"My mother's biggest weakness is my father. . . .
He's a slob!"
Sam, age 8

"She gives crummy piggyback rides."
Casey, age 6

"Hot buttered popcorn. We got to hide
it from her."
Jim, age 8

"My mother gives in too much to my father. She should wear more pants in the family."

Alison, age 8

If a Tabloid Ran a Headline About Mom

"LOCAL MOM TRIES TO GET SON TO STAY OUT
OF THE DIRT, BUT GIVES UP WHEN SON FINDS
TEN DOLLARS IN THE DIRT."
Paul, age 9

"LIZ TAYLOR CALLS MY MOTHER FOR ADVICE
ABOUT MARRIAGE."
Janet, age 10

"NATIONAL SCANDAL! MOM AND DAD ARE GETTING
ALONG TOO GOOD!"
Frieda, age 8

"MOTHER CAUGHT SAYING 'DARN,' BUT THAT'S THE ONLY
SWEAR WORD SHE SAYS."
Sean, age 8

"The newspaper in the grocery store
might say something like:
MRS. BROWN HAS GAINED FIFTEEN POUNDS!"
Will, age 7

"LADY WITH THREE KIDS MAY RUN FOR PRESIDENT.
PEOPLE MAY VOTE FOR HER ONCE THEY
TASTE HER PECAN PIE!"
Maura, age 9

"MOTHER ACCUSES DAUGHTER OF LOSING
HER EARRINGS BUT THEN FINDS THEM
UNDER THE TOILET."
Cheryl Ann, age 9

"MOM GETS BIG MOTHER'S DAY SURPRISE. SHE'S
PREGNANT AGAIN."
Yolanda, age 8

"MOM MAKES GREAT MATZOH BALL SOUP. . . . FAMILY ALWAYS
EATS IT AT CHRISTMASTIME."

Carey, age 7

"To be a good mother you should practice a lot
in front of the mirror."
Ken, age 9

Concerning the Relationship Between Mothers and Food

"Food is one way they show you they love you.
Another way is by helping you with your homework.
But the best way they show you is when they
give you a big hug."
Caroline, age 8

"Some mothers like to eat, but some are real skinny. . . . It all depends on their metabolisms and whether they can take what those diets dish out."

Steven, age 10

"It's kind of like they were all born knowing how to cook. It's almost like a miracle."

Julio, age 9

"They like to make you scrambled eggs in the morning, especially in the winter when you got to go out and wait for the bus. Those mothers are good in all weathers, though."

Bernie, age 8

Vignettes About Mom's Legendary Baking

"My mom's cookies are good weapons. The Ninja Turtles could use them."

Russ, age 8

"She makes some orange kind of cake, but my opinion is that it's a waste of the oranges nature gave us."

Arnold, age 10

"She doesn't have much time to bake, so we get
that Sara Lee company to do it for us."

Betsy, age 8

"The butcher, the baker, the candlestick maker. . . .
My mother doesn't do any of those."

Jasmine, age 9

"My mom should open up a bakery. Her lemon pie
is the best. Except when my dad helps.
Then it's just a lemon!"

Angela, age 10

"Her cookies used to be so good. But now we just get fat-free and cholesterol-free ice cream. . . . I say bring back the good old days."

James, age 10

Concerning Mom and Her Housekeeping Habits

"My mother is weird. She thinks that cleaning the house is the greatest thing since sliced bread."
James, age 10

"She is a neat freak. I think she needs to take up knitting so she'll calm down."
Rachel, age 8

"My mother is a real great person. She is the only person I ever met who can get my father to clean anything."

Tony, 10

"She makes up a name for every room that we got to clean. Mine is 'Operation Disaster.'"

Jan, age 8

"My opinion is that a neat house is a boring house. . . . Of course, my mother has a different opinion."

Tom, age 10

The Most Unusual Thing
About Mom

"She wants to keep a pony in her bedroom."
Sam, age 8

"Can you believe that my mother doesn't know
where a linebacker lines up in football? She needs to
learn more about the real world."
Michael, age 9

"One thing that is unusual is that she still believes in the tooth fairy. . . . She always tells me to put my tooth under the pillow for that fairy to see, so I can get some cash or a present."

Brian, age 7

"Sometimes she just gets up and dances for no reason."
Randi, age 8

Classic Mother's Day Cards

Happy Mother's Day, Mom
You're the best mom I ever had.
I hope you end up rich so you can buy me the
Barbie mansion.
Love,
Karen, age 8

Dear Mom,
So what if you're fat like a dinosaur.
You're still the greatest.
Happy Mother's Day.
Your little aggravation,
Mitchell, age 8

To Mom,
If I had enough money, I would get you a present.
But I don't. So here is a cupcake.
It's only mooshed a little.
Love,
Teddie, age 5

Mother,
I won't tell Dad you just lost a hundred dollars on
lottery tickets. But that was a dumb way
to spend Mother's Day.
Ryan, age 7

Dear Mummy,
Want to make a deal? You clean up my room for
me and I'll start listening to you.
What do you say?
Greetings,
Dick, age 7

Dear Mother,
You are the best mother a kid could have.
I think you are beautiful. And you are very kind too.
I hope I turn out to be as good a mother as you.
I want to make you a proud grandma
with no gray hairs or worries.
Love,
Jenny, age 8

A Few of Mom's Favorite Things

"Hairspray might be what she has the most of."
Ben, age 6

"She has a dinner set that she likes a whole bunch,
but we don't use it unless somebody important
comes over . . . like my dad's mother."
Anita, age 9

"She likes tight jeans. She thinks they make her look younger. . . . I got my own ideas about it."

Alexia, age 8

"My mother's favorite thing is exactly seven years old and cute as anything. . . . It's me! But don't tell my sister."

Ivan, age 7

"She's a big expert on art and that's why she appreciates the beautiful pictures I draw at school."

Marcy, age 7

What All Mothers Do When a Child Isn't Feeling Well

"Mothers get real worried, and they keep coming into your bedroom to see how you are. . . . Dads just say things like 'Don't worry, Phyllis. Junior will be up and Adam by tomorrow.' "

Jim, age 8

"Sometimes mothers say a prayer and they ask God to plug up the sneezing and the coughing. . . .
To tell you the truth, cough medicine can be a big help too."

Daniel, age 7

"If you have a big temperature, they get all sweaty and worried. That's the time to hit them for the new toy you want."

Dick, age 7

"If you have a real serious problem, they'll make you hot chocolate."

Patty, age 7

"I think all mothers should learn how to scuba dive, because you know how they all love those pearls."
Bradley, age 10

Helpful Suggestions for What Mothers Should Do in Their Spare Time

"She should get a real job and earn some extra money. . . . Her son will love her for it because he might need some freedom."

Dick, age 7

"Some mothers like to make pâté, but I think it's disgusting."

Ryan, age 7

"There's nothing like a little bungee jumping to clear your head."
Arnold, age 10

"They should be slaves to their children. The children should act like kings and the mothers should bring them fruit and soda."
Ken, age 9

"Mothers should use those tanning machines. It will help them relax and get dark without getting burnt. Besides, they sell gum and candy there, so I wouldn't complain if I had to wait."
Krista, age 7

Do Children Tend to Be Like Their Mothers?

"Girls look like their mothers, and boys are bossy just like their mothers."

Rachel, age 8

"I think that some children rebel and act more like that lady Cher."

Maura, age 9

"Well, you can learn a lot from your mother . . .
such as how to get your father to take you
to the mall."
Stacy, age 9

"There ain't nuthin' wrong with being like your
mother. Mine is good at Wiffle ball and
shootin' pool."
Phil, age 7

"A lot of times you do end up the same. Like my
mother is real pretty and I look something like her,
except for one thing that is different —I'm a whole
bunch of inches shorter."
Deborah, age 7

Concerning How Mothers Change
Once They Reach Fifty

"Mothers are always acting young even if they are plenty over-the-hill."

Maura, age 9

"They don't change too much. Even when they're fifty, they'll still tell you to wear a hat and a scarf. They just do it because they're supposed to."

Caroline, age 8

"I don't think they comb their hair as much, but they probably wash it just as much."
Nikki, age 6

"Their perfume might smell different because they had it saved in the closet for a long time."
Dick, age 7

"They still eat corn flakes, so there's no change."
Bo, age 8

"Some woman who has an *S* on her dress."
Arnold, age 10

Original Descriptions of a "Supermom"

"A lady who needs to be in bed by eight-thirty because she's all tired out from chasing her family around."

Anita, age 9

"It's a mother with a warm smile and good brains, because who else is going to teach a kid about life?"

Alison, age 8

"A supermom is usually married to a superdad. But in case she isn't, she might have a good career she can count on."

Stacy, age 9

"A supermom is the kind of mom who can fly. . . . Mine can't, but she jumps good when she does aerobics tapes."

Ryan, age 7

The Children's Advice to All New Mothers

"Have redheaded kids if you can. They are
a bundle of joy."
Rachel, age 8

"Mothers, don't have no girls! They're boring! Don't
take no offense though."
Dick, age 7

"It's okay to change your name to your husband's name. But if your name is Smith and his is Yuckypoo, you better keep the Smith and make sure your children are called Smith too. Because if their last name is Yuckypoo, they'll get beat up at school."

Jenny, age 8

"New mothers should all take singing lessons, because a lot of them will be humming those lullabies, and those babies might be little, but they aren't deaf. . . . Know what I mean?"

Arnold, age 10

"Motherhood is not for everybody—it's
only for ladies."

Harold, age 6

"Be a mother. It's a rewarding thing. Mothers and
Christmas are the two best things in the world. . . .
But my mother is the best gift I ever got."

Marie, age 9

Concerning What a Person Would Miss Out on if She Doesn't Get the Opportunity to Be a Mother

"Eating Girl Scout cookies. . . . But the bad side of it
is you got to buy a lot of them too."
Nancy, age 9

"Being in labor for forty-eight hours."
Paul, age 9

"You would never get the chance to spank a
naughty kid like me."
Jay, age 5

"Taking your kid for his first day of school."
Ricky, age 6

"You wouldn't get the chance to share those bagels
with raisins in them with your children."
Marcy, age 7

"You might not ever change those nasty, nasty,
stinky diapers. . . . Yeech!"
Daniel, age 7

"You'll miss out on knowing what cartoons to watch
on Saturdays."
Jeri, age 6

"You won't get to see the smile on your parents' faces when they find out they are grandparents."
Cheryl Ann, age 9

"You will miss a bunch of fun. You can have a good time. . . . Motherhood is fun! It's being the kid that's the hard part!"
Jordan, age 8

"You will not have the opportunity to be loved. . . . You won't know that you are loved by a child who is a really big fan of yours."

Marilyn, age 8

On Why Mothers Are the Most Important People in the World

"Because they take you caroling in December and that is an important contribution to the world."
Jenna, age 10

"Because mothers cook a whole lot better than fathers."
Alison, age 8

"Mothers are good at everything, but they shouldn't let it go to their heads."

Roger, age 8

"Mothers teach you how to talk. If it wasn't for them, you wouldn't be able to blab with your friends on the telephone."

Maura, age 9

"Mothers are more important than the President because they make laws at home that you really got to obey."

Bonnie, age 9

"Mothers are responsible for most of the new ideas in the world, such as having people wear clothes at the beginning of time. In the more modern years, they are the ones who probably thought up things like pillows and comforters and stuffed animals. We owe them a lot."

Lawrence, age 9

"Mothers bring you into life, and then they teach you that life isn't as tough as it looks sometimes."

Corinne, age 9

"They kiss you more than anybody else. . . . At least until you get married. But I'm not even thinking about that yet, since I got to get an education first."
Ruth, age 7

"Mothers are experts on the word that begins with *L* and ends with *E*."
Demi, age 8

"It sure would be hard to have children without them."
Kimberly, age 7

ABOUT THE AUTHOR

DAVID HELLER is widely known for his popular books about how children perceive the world and experience spirituality. He graduated from Harvard University and holds a Ph.D. in psychology from the University of Michigan. His work has appeared on ABC's *20/20* and in *People, Good Housekeeping, Psychology Today,* and *USA Today.*